Island Dreams

Okami Coloring Book

www.okamibooks.com

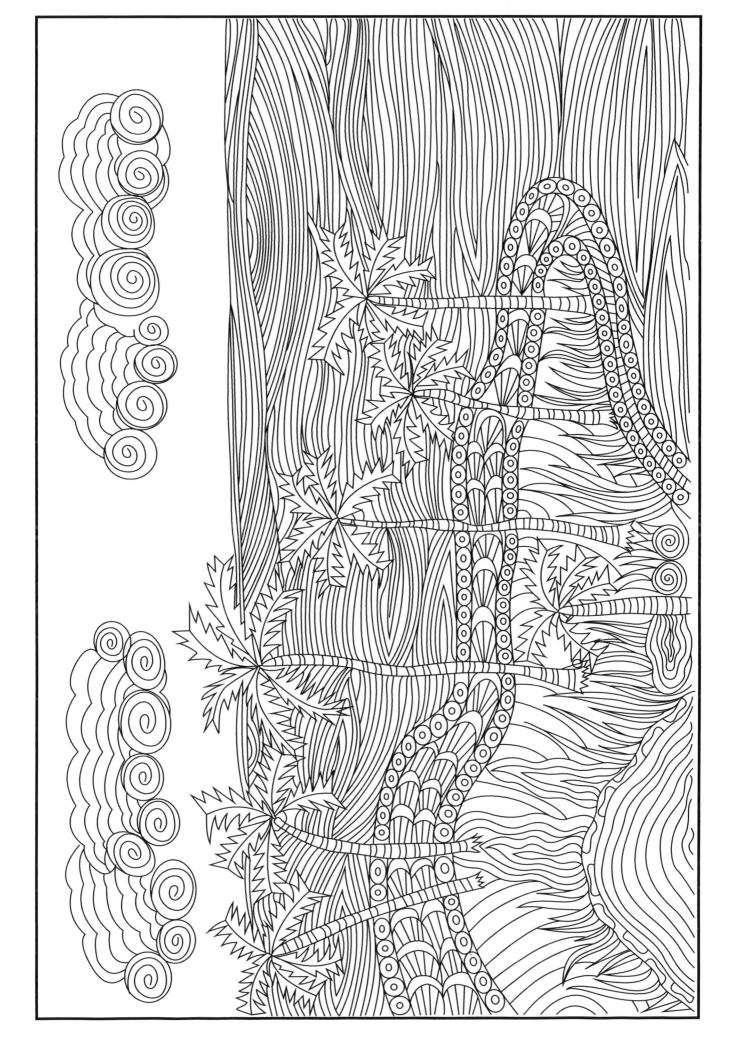

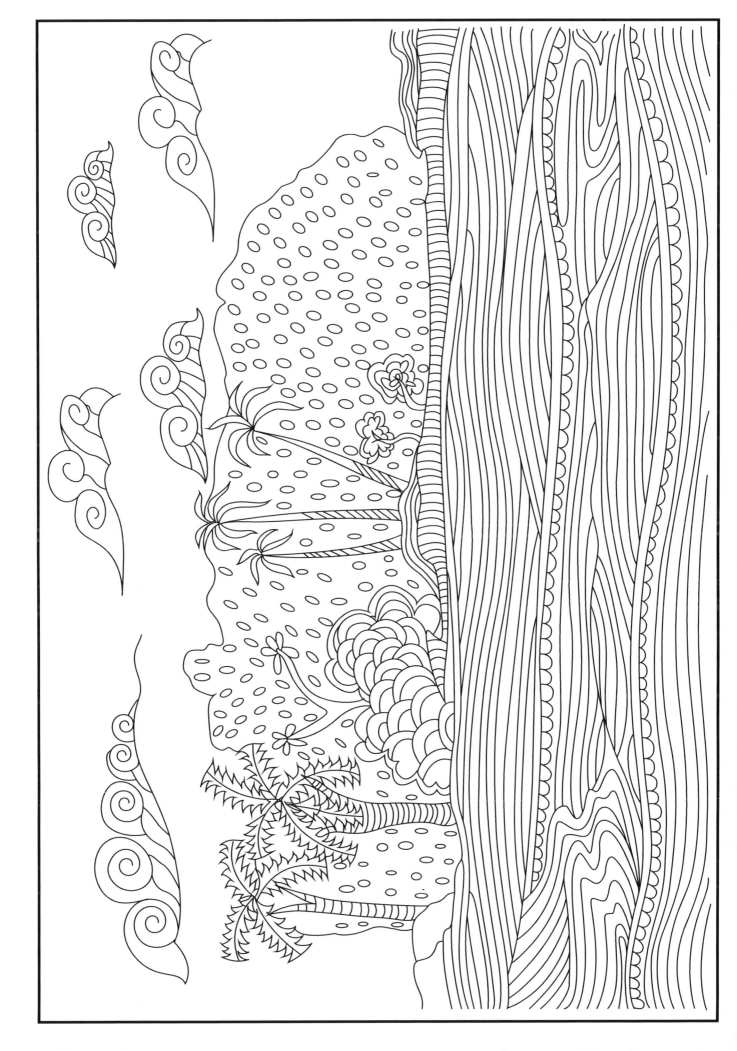

Coloring Books from Okami Books

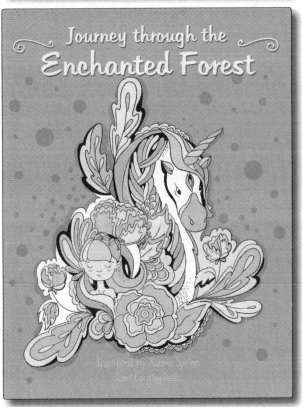

Subscribe to the newsletter to receive free coloring pages, as well as updates about upcoming promotions and free stuff.

www.okamibooks.com

Fantastic Ocean
Coloring Book

Illustrated by Ksenia Spirina

Okami Books

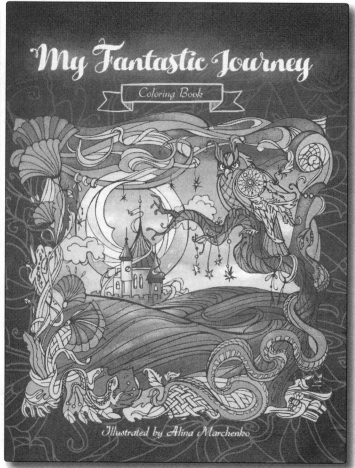

My Fantastic Journey
Coloring Book

Illustrated by Alina Marchenko

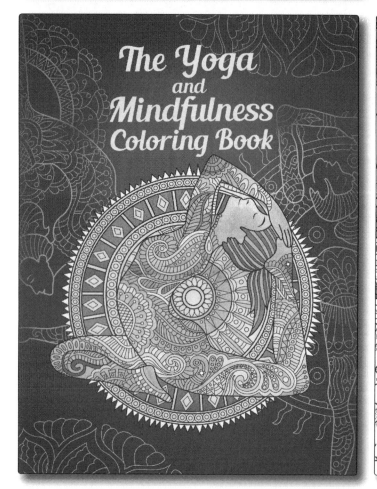

The Yoga
and
Mindfulness
Coloring Book

DOODLES
in
OUTER
SPACE

ILLUSTRATED BY IRVIN RAÑADA

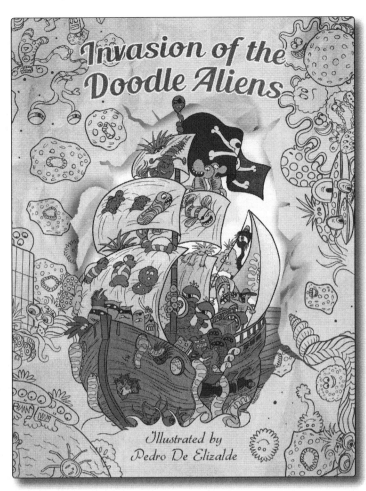

Invasion of the Doodle Aliens

Illustrated by
Pedro De Elizalde

Okami Books

The Hidden Spirits of the Enchanted Forest

Coloring Books

Illustrated by Forest Diver

International Delicacies

Illustrated by Ksenia Spirina

Okami Coloring Books

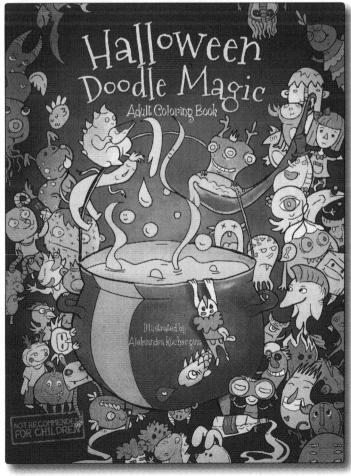

Halloween Doodle Magic

Adult Coloring Book

Illustrated by
Aleksandra Kochergina

NOT RECOMMENDED
FOR CHILDREN

Children's Books from Okami Books

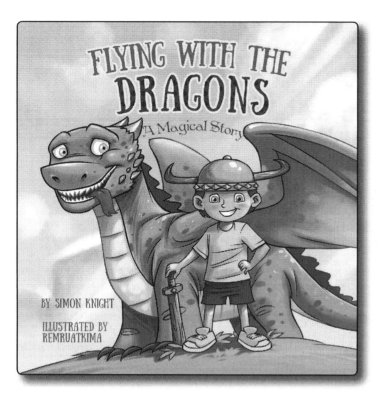

Subscribe to the newsletter to receive free coloring pages, as well as updates about upcoming promotions and free stuff.

www.okamibooks.com